KNOW THE GAME COMPLETE SKILLS
RUGBY

SIMON JONES

BLOOMSBURY
LONDON • NEW DELHI • NEW YORK • SYDNEY

Contents

Part One:
Passing, Catching and Kicking

When using this book, concentrate on one coaching point at a time. Practise each point until you have mastered it before moving on to the next one.
You do not need to work through the book from cover to cover. Choose a skill you want to work on and practise it until you are happy with the outcome.

Part Two:
Tackling, Contact, Teamwork, Tactics

PART ONE: PASSING, CATCHING AND KICKING

Do you want to play professional rugby, earning fame and fortune? Perhaps you can imagine playing rugby for your country in front of thousands of people, or maybe you just want to play the game well and enjoy it.

Whatever your ambitions, you need to start by learning some very important basic skills (called key skills) and, if you become really good at them, it will allow you to play the best rugby you can.

This book is designed to help you progress by providing a series of key skills. These include passing, catching and kicking practices that you can do in your back garden or a nearby open space, either on your own, with a friend, or with your brother, sister, mum or dad!

All you need is a rugby ball (size 3 or 4 are the best sizes until you are a teenager) and something to mark out a small area – it could be your hat, scarf or jumper if you have nothing else.

You need to practise each skill regularly, even after you become good at it! This book will show you ways to challenge yourself by making practices harder.

Please remember that, because the rugby ball is shaped like an egg, when it bounces it can go in any direction. This is part of the fun, but you should be careful to practise where the ball won't cause any damage or go into a road if it bounces in an unexpected direction.

WHAT MAKES A GOOD RUGBY PLAYER?

- Concentration
- Confidence
- Fitness
- Quick reactions and foot movement
- Good handling of the ball
- Ability to 'read' the game and adapt accordingly
- Courage

SCORING IN RUGBY

To win a game you need to score more points than the opposing team, and you need to be able help your team to score those points. You can only score points in the following four ways:

1 Touching the ball down behind the opposition try line = 5 points (called a try).
2 Kicking the ball (which is placed on the ground) between the posts and over the cross bar after a try has been scored (called a conversion) = 2 points.

The kick has to be taken in line with where the try was scored.
3 Kicking the ball through the posts but above the cross bar with the ball placed on the ground when your team has been awarded a penalty = 3 points.
4 Kicking the rugby ball between the posts on the half volley (called a drop goal) = 3 points.

The posts in rugby look like the letter "H" with two upright posts and a cross bar between them.

Rugby is a highly exciting game, full of energy and pace.

RUGBY **TERMS**

There are some words in rugby that mean nothing to most people, but rugby players and fans all over the world know exactly what they mean – it's like a special language which belongs just to rugby! Here is a list of words or terms that you can learn:

FORWARDS
These are the players (1 to 8) who try to get the ball at set pieces (see below).

SET PIECE
A scrum, line out or kick off.

SCRUM
The scrum is a means of restarting play after a stoppage that has been caused by a mistake, such as a forward pass or a knock on (see below). Having a scrum gets all the forwards in one place on the field, and this means there is space for the backs to run.

KNOCK ON
When a player drops or knocks the ball so it goes forward on to the ground.

During a ruck players will be fighting for possession of the ball.

In a maul, one of the players will have hold of the ball.

FORWARD PASS
When a player passes the ball forwards to a teammate.

LINE OUT
The line out is a way of restarting the game after the ball has gone into touch (off the field of play at the side). Like the scrum, the line out gets all the forwards in one place near to the touch line, so the backs have space to run in.

BACKS
These are the players who receive the ball from the forwards and they try to run and score.

THREE QUARTERS
Another name for the Backs.

RUCK
A ruck is when a group of players are trying to push each other off a ball on the ground in order to gain possession.

MAUL
This is the same as a ruck only this time one of the group will be holding the ball.

TOUCH LINE
The line which runs up the side of the pitch.

TRY LINE
The line which runs across the end of the pitch.

BE THE BEST
Learning these terms by heart will help to improve your skills, as you will be able to concentrate fully on your coach's instructions instead of struggling to work out what he is talking about!

POSITIONS IN **RUGBY**

There are 15 players in the usual rugby team, although there are fewer players in some versions of rugby. Seven-a-side is an exciting game, with its own World Cup, and there is also a 10-a-side game. Young players have fewer members on each team so that there is more chance to run with the ball. Here we will look at the positions in 15-a-side rugby.

A rugby team is split into forwards and backs. The Forwards contest for the ball with the opposition team's Forwards and then give it to their Backs, who try to get past the opposition players to score. Backs tend to be a little lighter than Forwards so that, if they win the ball, they can run fast.

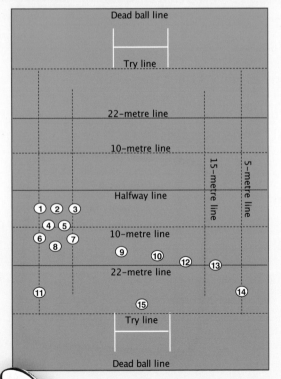

FORWARDS
No.	Name
1	Loosehead Prop
2	Hooker
3	Tighthead Prop
4	Lock or Second Row
5	Lock or Second Row
6	Blindside Flanker
7	Openside Flanker
8	Number Eight

BACKS
No.	Name
9	Scrum Half
10	Fly Half
11	Wing
12	Inside Centre
13	Outside Centre
14	Wing
15	Fullback

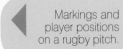

Markings and player positions on a rugby pitch.

Let's look at what each position requires:

1 LOOSEHEAD PROP

- Is strong in the scrum and so helps the Hooker.
- Is a strong support player at the line out.
- Is a strong tackler – tackles the man and the ball.
- Has the ability to stay on his feet and pass in contact.
- Pushes hard at the rucks and mauls.

2 HOOKER

- Can throw in to the lineout accurately.
- Wins the ball in the scrum.
- Runs around the pitch quickly.
- Is a strong runner with the ball.
- Is the boss of the scrum.

3 TIGHTHEAD PROP

- Is the strong man (the rock) of the scrum.
- Is a strong runner with the ball over short distances.
- Normally a 'square-shaped' player – big shoulders and strong legs.
- Has the ability to stay on his feet and pass in contact.
- Is a strong tackler – tackles the man and the ball.

4 & 5 LOCKS (SECOND ROW)

- Has the ability to jump in line out.
- Is fast around the pitch.
- Is a strong physical presence.
- Is an aggressive defender.

You need to be a strong runner to be a Hooker, like England star Lee Mears.

6 BLINDSIDE FLANKER

- Line out option – can jump.
- Is a strong runner with the ball.
- Has a huge work-rate.
- Is a good defender.

7 OPENSIDE FLANKER

- Dominates tackle and collision areas.
- Links forwards and backs.
- Is an extremely fit, fast player.
- Is a skilful ball player who wins the ball in rucks and mauls.

8 NUMBER EIGHT

- Has a huge work-rate.
- Is a good defender.
- Is a strong communicator and decision-maker.
- Is a strong runner with the ball.
- Understands and plans team options.

9 SCRUM HALF

- Is a quick, long, accurate passer.
- Has a huge work rate.
- Is the 'general' of the forwards.
- Is an accurate kicker.
- Understands all the team moves.

10 FLY HALF

- Is an accurate and quick passer with both hands.
- Is a threat to opposition defensive lines.
- Has all-round good kicking skills.
- Is a good decision-maker under pressure.
- Is one of the team leaders.

11 & 14 WING

- Is a very fast runner.
- Is good at scoring tries.
- Is good at swerving/side-stepping.
- Can ead the other team's defence and defends accurately.
- Can catch a high ball under pressure.
- Can kick well under pressure.

12 & 13 CENTRE

- Is a sharp and evasive runner.
- Is fast over 20 metres.
- Is a good kicker.
- Is a good passer off both hands.

15 FULL BACK

- Has kicking skills with either foot.
- Can catch a high ball under pressure.
- Is a fast and strong runner.
- Can run into space in attack.
- Communicates defence and defends accurately.

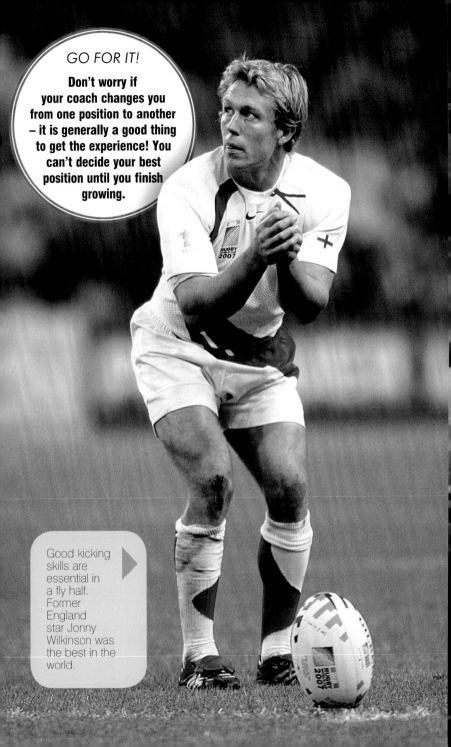

GO FOR IT!

Don't worry if your coach changes you from one position to another – it is generally a good thing to get the experience! You can't decide your best position until you finish growing.

Good kicking skills are essential in a fly half. Former England star Jonny Wilkinson was the best in the world.

PASSING

Whatever position you play, you will need to be able to pass the ball quickly and accurately. It is one of the basic skills of rugby – and it is not quite as simple as it looks. Top players practise all the time to perfect their passing and their ability to catch the ball, often when running at speed. Use these drills to help you become a reliable passer and catcher.

Passing practice
You will need:
- Two or three players.
- A rugby ball.
- A small area (10 paces by 10 paces).

Key points
- Run around the area in any direction passing the ball between each other.

- How many passes can you make in 30 seconds while staying at least 2 metres away from each other?
- Try to pass using your fingers behind the ball to flick it to your partner. This makes the ball go faster.
- Try different ways of passing: catch and pass the ball with your hands above your head, or catch and pass the ball with your hands below your knees.
- How many can you do without dropping the ball?

DID YOU KNOW?

England fly half Jonny Wilkinson is the only player to score in two World Cup finals... against Australia in 2003 and South Africa in 2007. He has also scored more than 1,000 points in Test matches for his country.

Make it harder
Instead of passing in any direction you now need to practise passing to the side and slightly behind you, as forward passes are not allowed in rugby.

Using the same small area try running alongside your partner across the area. The ball carrier

Lateral pass: The most common pass used in rugby.

should be slightly in front. When the pass is made, the player with the ball runs slightly faster so that they are in front of the player who just passed the ball. The player who just passed the ball should slow up a little to allow the new ball carrier to overtake him.

LATERAL (SIDEWAYS) PASS

This pass is the most common and is used when you pass the ball to a team mate running alongside and just behind you.

Remember to slow slightly after you have passed the ball.

Key points
- Run straight, holding the ball in two hands.
- Look at the player who will receive the pass.
- Swing your arms towards him and follow through so that your fingers on both hands end up pointing towards the receiver.
- Pass the ball at chest height in front of the receiver.

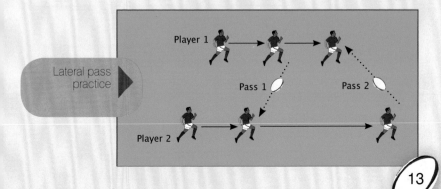

Lateral pass practice

Player 1

Pass 1   Pass 2

Player 2

- Support the new ball carrier (i.e. be within passing distance in case he needs to pass the ball).

RUNNING AND PASSING

- Run straight – if you run across the pitch you may not be going forwards!
- Hold the ball in both hands – if you hold it under one arm you cannot pass properly.
- Commit a defender – run towards the left side of the defender if you are passing to the right (see diagram opposite) so that the defender is drawn across, which creates space for your teammate to run into.
- Turn your upper body side-on to the defence, to face the supporting receiver.
- Swing your arms through in the direction of the pass.
- Use your elbows and wrists to control the speed and flight of the ball as it is released.
- Follow through with your hands in the direction of the pass.
- Pass to the 'target' area, which is at chest height in front of the receiver.
- Support the receiver once the pass has been completed by remaining in passing distance.

Running and passing: Swing your arms through in the direction of the pass.

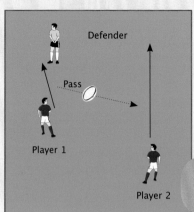

Defender

Pass

Player 1

Player 2

When you are running and passing, commit a defender by running to his left if you are passing to the right.

CATCHING A PASS

- Position yourself so that you can run towards the ball in its flight.
- Run towards the space created by the passer drawing the defender towards him.
- Call for the ball.
- Reach with your hands to catch the ball early.
- Watch the ball into your hands.
- Catch the ball with your fingers and hands.
- Get ready to pass to another member of your team.

SPIN PASS

If you make the ball spin when you pass it, it will travel further and faster through the air. But it can also make the ball harder to catch, so only use a spin pass when you want to pass over a longer distance than normal. The best example of this is the scrum half pass (see page 16).

Key points

- Hold the ball in both hands with the point facing up.
- Put your hands on either side of the ball so that you are holding it at its widest part.
- Throw the ball about half a metre into the air and catch it again.
- Use your strong hand (right if you are right handed) to 'roll' the ball as it leaves your hands.
- Repeat this until you can throw the ball high so that it spins in the air and lands in your hands without tumbling – the ball should spin around but should stay with the point-up.

Now, stand facing a partner and pass to each other so the ball spins as it did when you were throwing it to yourself.

Key points

- Position yourself exactly as you would for a lateral pass.
- Hold the ball so the point is facing towards the receiver.
- Look at the player who will receive the pass.
- Swing your arms towards him and let the ball roll out of your right hand (if you are passing to the left) or left hand (if you are passing to the right).
- Follow through with the fingers of both your hands, so that they finish up pointing towards the receiver.
- Pass the ball at chest height in front of the receiver.

Make it harder

- Start a metre or so away. Every time you both catch the ball move one step backwards.
- If one of you drops the ball take one step towards each other.
- See how far you can pass it without dropping the ball.
- Then run across a small area passing sideways to each other, as you did with the lateral pass, but gradually move further away from each other.

OVERHEAD PASS

Sometimes in a game you may need to pass the ball over the head(s) of players to one of your teammates who is in space and has no one in front of him. This is called an overhead pass.

You will need:
- Three players.
- A rugby ball.
- A small area (10 paces by 10 paces).

Practice

- Run around the area in any direction, passing the ball between two of you with the third player trying to catch the ball (piggy in the middle).

DID YOU KNOW?

England, Ireland, Scotland and Wales compete with France and Italy every year in a tournament known as the Six Nations. Each team plays five matches, and winning every match is known as a Grand Slam.

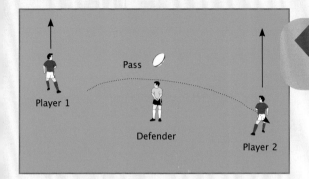

Player 1

Pass

Defender

Player 2

Practising the overhead pass: It's like piggy in the middle.

- The receiver needs to keep moving so that the player in the middle can't get between you.
- If the player in the middle catches the ball or it is dropped, swap the player in the middle.

- Try to make the pass using your fingers to spin the ball to your partner.
- Now try to pass over the head of the player in the middle, but remember that the receiver still has to move around.

Overhead pass.

SCRUM HALF PASS

This is called a scrum half pass because the scrum half uses this pass the most as the link between the forwards and the backs.

During a game of rugby, however, there are often occasions when a group of players are all in one part of the field together, normally in a ruck or a maul. The player arriving last to the group will need to pass the ball, maybe from the ground, away quickly and over some distance to a teammate. Therefore, every player on the team needs to be able to pass the ball this way, from a position that is low to the ground.

Practice 1
You will need:
- Two of you – if you are on your own you can use a wall to pass against.
- A rugby ball.

Key points
- Put the ball on the ground so that the point is facing in the direction you are passing.

Scrum half pass: Crouch low to pick up the ball from the ground. Remember to follow through with both arms so that they end up pointing towards the receiver.

- Put your rear foot beside the ball – it should be your right foot if you are passing to your left.
- Make sure your feet are wide apart so that you can get down to the ball.
- Put both your hands on the wide part of the ball with the point pointing in the direction you want to pass.
- Sweep the ball towards your target (the hands of the receiver or a point on a wall if you are on your own).
- Let the ball roll off the fingers of your right hand (if passing to the left) or left hand (if passing to the right).
- Follow through with the fingers of both your hands so that they end up pointing towards the receiver.
- Pass the ball at chest height in front of the receiver.

Make it harder
- Try to sweep the ball away from you as soon as you touch it (without picking it up and moving it backwards before you pass).
- Increase the distance you are passing.
- Get the receiver to run on to your pass. You will need to pass in front of him.

Practice 2
If there are three of you, you will need:
- A rugby ball
- Four cones or markers (you can use anything that isn't sharp).

Key points
- Mark out a square with a marker on each corner.
- Each of you stands on a different corner, leaving one free.
- One of you has the ball at your feet.
- Make a scrum half pass to the nearest player, then run in the opposite direction to the spare corner (see photos opposite).
- The next player does the same thing – passing one way and then running the other.

19

As soon as you pass the ball, run to the next cone.

Make it harder

- Try to pass around the square four times without dropping the ball.
- Time yourselves – how many passes can you make in 30 seconds or one minute, for example?
- Increase the distance you are passing by making the square bigger.

French scrum half Morgan Parra gathers the ball from a scrum and executes a perfect scrum half pass. Notice his grip on the ball.

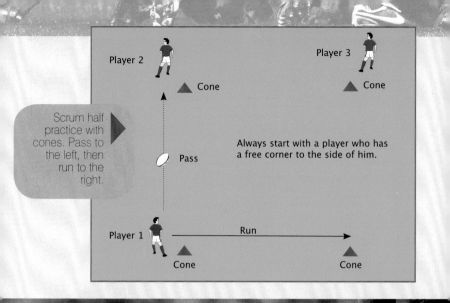

Player 2

Player 3

▲ Cone

▲ Cone

Scrum half practice with cones. Pass to the left, then run to the right.

🏉 Pass

Always start with a player who has a free corner to the side of him.

Player 1 ————— Run ————→

▲ Cone

▲ Cone

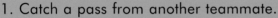

CATCHING

Rugby is a handling game, which means that you will need to be good at catching the ball. You may need to:

1. Catch a pass from another teammate.
2. Intercept a pass made by the opposition.
3. Catch a kick made by either a teammate or the opposing team.

CATCHING A HIGH BALL

You will need:
• Just you to start with.
• A rugby ball.

Key points
• Without a ball, point your hands up to the sky, stretching them above your head. If you move your bottom hand out a little way from your body this will give you the best position for catching a high ball.
• Now hold a rugby ball in both hands and make sure you have plenty of space around you.
• Throw the ball up above your head and catch it as it comes down by reaching both your hands up towards the ball, remembering the first position.

1

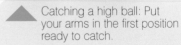

Catching a high ball: Put your arms in the first position ready to catch.

- See if you can catch the ball by pulling it down rather than letting it hit your hands.
- See if you can catch the ball softly, without it making a sound.

GO FOR IT!

Throw the ball a little higher each time you practise, making sure you catch the ball softly. See how high you can go.

 Pull the ball in rather than letting it hit your hands.

 Receive the ball into your body, ready to pass to another player.

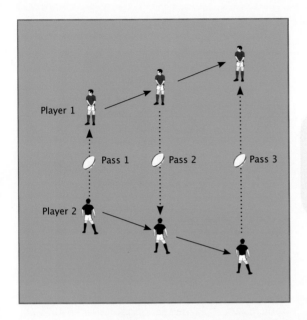

Player 1

Pass 1 Pass 2 Pass 3

Player 2

Catching practice with a partner. See if you can move further apart .

Make it harder

- Ask a partner to join you and take turns throwing the ball up to each other.
- Gradually move further apart, but be careful to make sure you have plenty of space around you both.
- Once you are catching the ball confidently, try a little competition. Each time you catch the ball move one step further apart. How far can you get before dropping the ball?
- Try this same competition, but punt kick the ball to each other instead (see page 29).

CATCHING A PASS IN THREES

You will need:
- A rugby ball.
- Two partners to practise with you.

Key points

- Stand in a line two metres away from each other, all facing in the same direction.
- Pass the ball to the middle player.
- The receiver reaches out so that he takes the ball early, spreading his fingers wide.

- Keep your eyes open and watch the ball until it is safely in his hands.
- The pass should be made at chest height.
- Now pass back and forth between the three of you, making sure that you all reach with both hands to pull the ball in rather than allowing it to hit your hands.
- When making a pass, swing your arms across your body and release the ball towards the receiver.
- If you are the player in the middle, can you catch the ball and pass it on in one swinging movement?

Make it harder
- Move a little further away.
- Once you are catching the ball confidently, try a competition. Each time you catch the ball move a step further apart. How far can you get without dropping the ball?
- Now try jogging together in line and passing the ball as you go.
- Gradually speed up, but be sure to pass backwards. The way to do this is to slow a little when you have made the pass and to speed up a little when you have the ball.
- Take turns to be the middle player. It is the hardest position, but gives you the best practice!

Catching a pass in threes.

KICKING

Although rugby is mainly a running and passing game, there are times when you need to kick. There are five main types of kick:

1 A drop kick: To start the game or to score three points.
2 A place kick: To score a conversion after a try has been scored (see page 3) or to kick a penalty.
3 Chip kick: To beat a defender by kicking over or around him.
4 A punt kick: A kick into space or to relieve pressure by finding touch (kicking the ball over the touch line).
5 A grubber kick: Kicking the ball along the ground to beat defenders or find space.

When practising your kicking you should remember to check the following:

• Make sure you have a strong pair of rugby boots on. Kicking with soft footwear may hurt your feet!

• The rugby ball bounces in odd directions because of its shape, so make sure you have plenty of space around you.
• Warm up before you start practising so that you don't injure yourself.

DID YOU KNOW?

The first ever international rugby match took place on March 27, 1871, in Edinburgh between Scotland and England. The hosts won.

DROP KICK
You will need:
• A rugby ball.
• Space to practise in.

Key points
• Hold the ball so that it points downwards with your hands on either side of it.

- Keep your head and shoulders still, and hold the ball over your foot so that the point of the ball is slightly towards you.
- Step forward and plant the foot that you are not kicking with firmly on the ground.
- Drop the ball on to its point on the ground.
- Kick the ball with the top of your foot just after it has hit the ground – too early and the ball will bump along the ground (see grubber kick on page 31) – too late and you will miss it.
- Swing your leg through the ball so it pops up into the air.

- Try to keep your balance by holding out the opposite arm to your kicking foot (right footed = left arm out for balance).
- Keep swinging your foot up after you have kicked the ball, and keep your head down until the ball is in the air.
- To start with, just practise kicking the ball a little way in the air.

Make it harder
- Have a bench or similar low target to kick over.
- Try to get the ball higher each time.

Drop kick: 1. Hold the ball above your foot.
2. Drop the ball and kick it just after it hits the ground, following through with your leg.

- Pick a higher target (such as a washing line, but check with your parents or guardians first), and try standing close to it, but still drop kick the ball over the target.

PLACE KICK

You will need:
- A rugby ball.
- A lot of space to practise in.

Key points
- Place the ball on the ground on a slightly raised mound of mud (you can use the heel of your boot to create this).
- Lean the ball slightly forwards, as this will give you the wide part of the ball (the sweet spot) to hit.
- Keeping your head and shoulders still, stand over the ball with your kicking foot behind the ball.
- Walk backwards a few paces. Keep your eye on the sweet spot of the ball.
- Take a few deep breaths and focus on the sweet spot.
- Walk forward to the ball and plant the foot that you are not kicking with firmly on the ground next to the ball.
- Turn the shoulder opposite to your kicking foot towards the target.

Place kick: Swing your kicking leg through the ball as you strike it, holding out your opposite arm to keep your balance.

GO FOR IT!

Improve the accuracy of your place kick by aiming for a target. How many times in a row can you kick the ball into your target area?

- Swing your kicking foot through the ball, keeping your head down.
- Sweep the ball away by hitting it with the inside of your foot.
- Keep your balance by holding out the arm opposite to your kicking foot.
- Keep swinging your foot up, even after you have kicked the ball, and keep your head down until the ball is in the air.
- To start with, just practise kicking the ball a little way with a two- or three-pace run up.

As you improve your place kick, try increasing the distance you aim for.

CHIP KICK

This is used to kick the ball over a defender's head. You should start by practising from a standing position.

Key points
- Keep your eyes on the ball.
- With your head and shoulders still, hold the ball over your foot so that the point of the ball is slightly towards you.
- Step forward and plant the foot that you are not kicking with firmly on the ground.
- Drop the ball on to your kicking foot with your dominant hand (your right hand if you are right-handed).
- Swing your leg through the ball so it pops up into the air.
- Try to keep your balance so that you don't fall over.
- Keep your foot pointing straight ahead, and don't tilt it up towards your head.

Chip kick:
1. Drop the ball on to your kicking foot and swing your leg through to meet it.
2. The ball should 'chip' through the air over the head of the defending player.
3. Keeping your eyes on the ball, run around the defender to gather it.

GO FOR IT!

**Try practising
the chip kick while
jogging. It will take a
few goes to get it right,
then you can start to
build up your
speed.**

around and catch it on the other side.
- If there are two of you, take turns being the defender. At first, the defender should not try to intercept the ball, but as the kicker gets more proficient the defender can try to stop it by raising his hands. Then the attacker needs to kick a little higher!

- Keep swinging your foot up even after you have kicked the ball, and keep your head down until the ball is in the air.
- To start with, just practise kicking the ball a little way in the air. See if you can catch it again without having to run too far ahead.

Make it harder
- See if you can walk along, kick the ball up and catch it again.
- Now try jogging – it will take quite a few goes to get this right.
- If you can, use a small bush or chair as a defender.
- Remember, start slowly and gradually build up your speed until you can run at the defender and pop the ball up with your foot and then run

PUNT KICK
This is similar to the chip kick, but you will be trying to get much more height and distance on the ball. Try to kick the ball towards a target, such as a jumper on the ground, but it should be no more than a few metres away to start with. Make sure there is plenty of room to practise your kicking and that there are no windows near by!

DID YOU KNOW?

**Former prop Jason
Leonard has played
in more international
matches than any other
Englishman. He won a
total of 114 caps in a
career spanning 14 years.**

Key points
- Put your hands on either side of the ball.
- Point the toe of your kicking foot.
- If you are kicking with your right foot, put your left shoulder forward.
- Place your non-kicking foot firmly on the ground, lined up towards your target.
- Drop the ball on to your foot as it swings through.
- Kick the ball towards the target before it drops too far.
- Hit the ball along its length and not at the point.
- Swing your kicking foot through after kicking the ball towards the target.
- Hold out the arm opposite your kicking foot to help you to keep your balance.

Make it harder
- See if you can make the ball travel higher by kicking it later as your foot swings through.
- Kick over a bench or a similar obstacle and see if you can still land the ball on the target.
- Move further away from the target, but make sure you keep landing the ball near it every time.
- If you can get a partner to join you, take turns kicking to each other and see how far you can move back before your kicking becomes inaccurate. This is a good way for you to practise your catching skills as well as improving your kicking.

Punt kick: 1. Pointing your toes, drop the ball on to your kicking foot.
2. Follow through your kick to improve the accuracy of your aim.

GRUBBER KICK

This is kicking the ball along the ground to beat a defender. Again, begin by practising this while you are standing still.

Key points

- Put your hands on either side of the ball.
- Point the toe of your kicking foot towards the ground.
- Make sure your weight is over the top of the ball.
- Drop the ball on to your foot as it swings through.
- Push the ball forwards on to the ground with a short, stabbing kick.
- Follow the kick through with your foot.
- The ball should bounce a metre or so in front of you before bouncing along the ground.

Make it harder

- Use a small bush or chair as a defender.
- Remember; start slowly and gradually build up your speed until you can run at the defender and stab the ball past him with your foot, then run around and catch it as it bounces along.
- If there are two of you, take turns being the defender.

Grubber kick: Kicking the ball along the ground to get around a defender.

33

Welcome to *Tackling, Contact, Teamwork, Tactics*. Rugby is a contact sport and in this book we will be looking at how to prepare yourself to manage contact without losing the ball or hurting yourself. You will also learn how to stop opposition players by tackling them – this is great fun, but you need to know what you are doing!

Rugby players need to work together as a team to beat the opposition. How do you out-think them? You need to use tactics so that you can plan to do what the opposition is least expecting. Like a general in battle, you are trying to out-fox the enemy. The difference is that after the battle we shake hands with the opposition!

DID YOU KNOW?

The game of rugby was invented in 1823 at Rugby school in Warwickshire when a boy named William Webb Ellis picked up the ball and ran with it. It is now played all over the world, and is particularly big in the Southern Hemisphere countries of Australia, New Zealand and South Africa.

In *Passing, Catching, Kicking* we looked at ways of scoring points by kicking penalties, conversions and drop goals. But rugby is essentially a running game and the main objective is to score a try by placing the ball on the ground over the opposition's try line.

You need to practise scoring a try. If you don't, you might drop the ball over the line (instead of placing it on the ground with downwards pressure), in which case all your hard work would be undone as the 'try' would be disallowed.

Here is a first simple practice for scoring a try.

 Rugby is a contact sport and you need to learn how to tackle correctly.

SCORING A TRY

Key points
- Run with the ball in two hands.
- As you cross an imaginary or real line, score a try by firmly placing the ball on the ground.

Make it harder
- Run on after you have put the ball down, leaving it on the ground. Look back – is it lying still on the ground in the same spot? In that case you have grounded it with downward pressure without dropping it and a try is scored. If it is moving, or has moved from the spot where you 'scored' it will not be given as a try and will instead be ruled as a 'knock on'. The opposing team is then given the ball.
- If the ground is soft enough and you don't mind getting muddy, see if you can dive on the ground over the line with the ball held in two hands into your chest.
- Go slowly, putting your knees on the ground first and then dropping down to the floor with your chest.
- Make sure the ball doesn't spill or get knocked out of your hands.
- Don't hold the ball into your tummy, or you may get the wind knocked out of you as you land on it!

 Scoring a try is the object of the game.

AVOIDING A **TACKLE**

You need to learn how to avoid being tackled as you run with the ball. If a defender tries to tackle you and there is no supporting player to pass to, you will need to use your own skills to get past the opposing player. There are a number of ways to beat a defender:

- Run around him. Be so quick that he can't catch you.
- Side-step him. Leave him tackling thin air!
- Swerve around him. Again, leave him trying to tackle the space that you have just run out of.
- Kick the ball past him. Then get it back before he can turn and get it himself.

RUN AROUND

If you can see that you have a slower player in front of you, don't be afraid to have a go at running around him.

Be careful that you don't run away from supporting players and end up getting tackled or running into touch (i.e. running off the pitch, causing the ball to be given to the other team)! Your teammates may be a little disappointed that you didn't pass to them, so the trick is to have a go, and if you see that you are not going to make it, slow up and look for support.

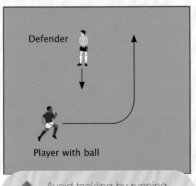

Defender

Player with ball

Avoid tackling by running around the opposing player.

THE SIDE-STEP

The side-step is used to fool the defender into trying to tackle the space he thought you were going to run into.

Key points

- Run towards the defender's inside shoulder – this is the left

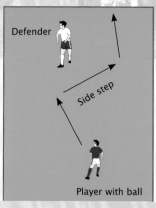

Defender

Side step

Player with ball

Practise avoiding a tackle by using the side-step.

shoulder if you are going to pass them on the right.

• Take short steps as you get near to the defender to help you get your timing and balance right.

• Change direction close to the defender by pushing sideways powerfully off the right foot to go left or the left foot to go right. In the diagram the ball carrier pushes off his left foot to go right.

• Think of your shoulders as the signal that fools the defender. Face them towards the way you want him to think you are going, but as you push off your front foot, turn them to face the new direction.

• You have to be quick to accelerate away while the defender is wrong-footed.

The side-step: 1. Run towards the defender, aiming for the side opposite the one you intend to pass him on.
2. Pretend to run to this side.
3. At the last second, quickly change direction and run round the opposite side.

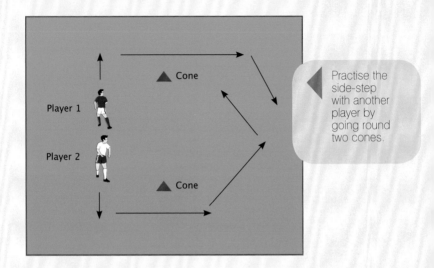

Practise the side-step with another player by going round two cones.

Practice

You will need:
- Just you to start with.
- A rugby ball.
- A marker on the ground to take the place of a defender.

Run up to the mark on the ground and follow the key points described on page 5.

Make it harder

- Ask a partner to join you and take turns being the defender.
- At first, the defender should stand still. Then you can make it more interesting by getting the defender to run as well.
- Use cones or jumpers as markers to run around.

THE SWERVE

The swerve is used to fool the defender into tackling the space he thought you were going to run into, just like the side-step. The difference is that you pivot or swing on one foot to fool the defender. It is most effective combined with a dummy pass.

Key points

- Run towards the defender's inside shoulder. This is the left shoulder if you are going to pass him to the right.
- Take short steps as you get near to the defender to help you get your timing and balance right.

- Change direction close to him by making a pass with your arms towards your supporting player. Then, just as you should let go of the ball, hold on to it and swing around your planted foot to run inside the defender.

The swerve: 1. Run towards the defender, aiming for the opposite side to the one you intend to go past him on. Just in front of the defender, pretend to make a pass to a supporting player.

2. Quickly pivot on your foot and turn in the opposite direction.

3. Accelerate away while the defender is wrong-footed.

39

TACKLING

The game of rugby is a contact game. This means that you will have to be good at physically stopping the opposing players by tackling them. The idea of the tackle is not just to stop the opposition player, but also to win the ball back.

It is essential that you only start practising the tackle after you have been coached in the basic techniques by a qualified coach.

Use these ideas to improve your technique away from team practices, but you should have an adult with you when you practise tackling.

BEING TACKLED

This is an important aspect of rugby to get right, as all players will be tackled during a game, and if you lose the ball you won't be very popular with your teammates! We will examine taking the ball into contact later in this book. For now, let's look at how, when you are tackled, you protect yourself and make sure the ball stays with your team.

FALLING IN THE TACKLE

When you are tackled and you are falling to the ground, the main thing to remember is not to put your hand out to stop your fall, which can lead to injury to your wrist, shoulder or arm. The best way to stop yourself from doing this is to hold the ball in two hands. As you fall, you should roll on to your hip and then your shoulder to break the fall, while you continue to hold the ball in both hands.

Key points
- As the tackler approaches you, try to keep low so that you are harder to tackle.
- Make sure you are holding the ball in both hands.
- Hold the ball away from the tackler by turning towards your own teammates (see more on page 42).

 Falling in the tackle:
1. Go down on your knees as if you were going to make a roll.
2. Fall sideways, landing on your hip.
3. Continue to fall letting your shoulder hit the ground.
4. Hold the ball out ready for your teammates to collect.

• Tuck your shoulder under and roll on to your upper back.

MAKING THE TACKLE

If you go into a tackle half heartedly it could mean that you are not in the correct position and you could get hurt, so it is important to start by practising tackling in stages. You need to be confident that you have mastered each stage before you progress to the next one (see photos opposite):

• Stay on your feet as long as possible.
• As you fall, roll on to the ground first rolling on to your knees, then your hip, and then your shoulder.

Stage 1
Start on your knees, with the ball carrier you are tackling on his knees as well.

Stage 2
The ball carrier holds the ball in both arms. Remember, he should not put his arm out to stop himself hitting the ground. Instead, he should roll on to the ground on to his hip and then shoulder.

Stage 3
Once you are comfortable with the technique, get the ball carrier you are tackling to 'walk' slowly past you, with both of you still on your knees.

Tackling stage 1: Get a partner and face each other on your knees.

Stage 2: Go for the tackle.

Stage 3: Down on the ground. Now repeat stages 1 and 2 while 'walking' on your knees.

Stage 4: Practise tackling from a crouch position.

Stage 5: Increase the pace with the ball carrier jogging.

Stage 4
Once you are comfortable with stages 1 to 3, have the ball carrier stand and walk past you while you are in a crouch position, ready to make the tackle.

Stage 5
Then have the ball carrier jog past you while you crouch and make the tackle.

Stage 6
When you are feeling confident, try it with both of you jogging.

Putting it all together
Make sure you have the correct technique at each stage before moving on. When you are ready you can try different types of tackle. There are three main types:
1 The side tackle
2 The front tackle
3 The rear tackle.

To practise the tackles you will need:
• A partner who is roughly the same size and weight as you.
• A rugby ball.
• A soft area to work on, such as grass or, if indoors, mats.

THE SIDE TACKLE

This tackle is made when you are running in to tackle the ball carrier from the side. The most important point to remember is to put your head behind the ball carrier and keep it there throughout the tackle – you don't want the ball carrier landing on your head!

Key points

- Make sure you are to the side of the ball carrier.
- As you go to make the tackle make sure your head will go behind the ball carrier – see photo 1.
- Make sure you have a low body position as you near the ball carrier.
- Keeping your eyes open, position your head behind, or to one side of, the ball carrier (cheek-to-cheek).
- Make contact with your shoulder on the ball carrier's thighs.
- Keep your chin up and your back straight.
- Squeeze your arms tight while driving with your legs.
- Roll to finish on top and get back to your feet quickly.

Side tackle: 1. Go in for the tackle making sure your head is behind the ball carrier's back.

2. Keeping a low position, tackle the ball carrier around the thighs.

3. Drive with your legs and roll.

Key points

- Fix your eyes on the hips of the ball carrier.
- Get low with your arms wide and be light on your feet, so that you can move sideways if the ball carrier tries to run around you.
- Go towards the ball carrier, staying low.
- Make contact with your shoulder just below the ball carrier's waist.
- Wrap your arms around the ball carrier's legs and squeeze.
- Drive with your legs to knock the ball carrier over.
- Make sure that you finish with your head on top of the ball carrier.
- Get back on your feet.

THE FRONT TACKLE

This tackle is made when an opposition player is running at you with the ball. It can be the most difficult tackle to make, but if you do it right it is very effective and can often result in your team winning back the ball.

To make it less intimidating, look at the player you are going to tackle. You are only tackling his legs and waist. His top half doesn't actually matter!

GO FOR IT!

After making your tackle, get back to your feet as quickly as possible. You need to pick up the ball and get it to your own teammates before the opposition supporting players arrive.

Front tackle: 1. Go in low with your arms wide.

2. Put your arms around the ball carrier's legs.

3: Squeeze with your arms and drive forwards to take the ball carrier down.

Rear tackle: 1. Go in for the tackle slightly to one side.

THE REAR TACKLE

This tackle is made when an opposition player is running away from you with the ball. You need to be quicker than him, which will often be the case when he is carrying the ball.

The key point here is to drive with your shoulder to knock him over. Remember, always finish with your head on top!

Key points

- Make sure you are slightly to the side of the ball carrier.
- As you go to make the tackle, make sure your head will go to the side of the ball carrier.
- Make sure you have a low body position as you get near the ball carrier.
- Keeping your eyes open, position your head to one side of the ball carrier (cheek-to-cheek).

2. Make contact at thigh-height with your head to the side.

3. Drive and twist to bring down the ball carrier.

No you don't: Gloucester's James Simpson-Daniel executes a fine rear tackle to stop Cardiff's Ben Blair in the 2009 EDF Trophy Final at Twickenham.

- Make contact with your shoulder on the ball carrier's thighs.
- Keep your chin up and your back straight.
- Squeeze your arms tight while driving with the legs.

- Twist and drive slightly sideways so that you land on top of the ball carrier, using him as a soft landing pad!
- Roll to finish on top and get back to your feet quickly.

CONTACT

We have looked at ways to avoid a tackle, but sometimes there is no alternative to carrying the ball into contact with the opposition. It is almost always a last resort, because it would normally be better to pass the ball before being tackled. This helps you to make ground and keep the ball away from the opposing team.

As soon as you get into contact you are taking the ball near to your opponents and they may be able to snatch the ball away from you unless you are careful! Therefore, try to keep the ball away from the opposing team as long as possible until your supporting players can arrive and help.

DID YOU KNOW?

The Southern Hemisphere countries of Australia, New Zealand and South Africa have their own equivalent of Europe's Six Nations tournament, called the Tri Nations.

The national teams are often referred to by their nicknames rather than their nationality – the Wallabies (Australia), the All Blacks (New Zealand) and the Springboks (South Africa).

TAKING THE BALL INTO CONTACT

The main thing to remember when taking the ball into contact is that you need to keep your body between the opposing players and the ball.

To help you, imagine the tackler is a small tree. His body is the trunk of the tree and therefore the strongest part; his arms are the branches and still quite a strong part of the tree; his fingers are the twigs and they are definitely the weakest part of the tree!

So which part do you want to run against if you can't get completely around and there is no one to pass to? His hands.

Allowing yourself to be tackled should always be the last resort.

Key points
- Stay light on your feet so that you move the defender to where you want him – not the other way around.
- Try to run to the side of the tackler – aim for the twigs!
- Keep your chin off your chest and your eyes open.
- Adopt a crouched position, ready to drive up into the tackler.
- Take a big, wide powerful step into contact.

- Keep your body between the defender and the ball.
- Keep your spine parallel to the ground and in line with the direction you are aiming for.

GOING TO GROUND
If your supporting players don't arrive quickly enough you may find yourself getting turned around and the opposing players could get their hands on the ball.

If you have no team support, you may have no choice but to go to ground.

To delay this as long as possible you will have to slide down on to the ground. You are creating a "ruck", (see page 21) which means the opposition cannot get the ball easily as they have to step over you to reach it while staying on their feet. If your supporting players arrive in time, they can knock the opposing players back off the ball and so secure possession.

(see page 21)

GO FOR IT!

Practise landing in a tackle so that you are facing your own team with your back towards the opposition. This will help your team keep possession.

Key points

- Avoid putting your arms out to break your fall. Try to land on your backside or back.
- Slide down the tackler to give yourself support.
- Body first, then ball. Do not throw the ball away. Hold it tightly until you are down on the ground.
- Look for support throughout, and try to pass off the ground

if there is a supporting player arriving.

- Place the ball with outstretched arms immediately away from you and towards your arriving teammates.

THE RUCK

A ruck is formed when the ball is on the ground and at least two players are bound together over the top contesting for the ball.

The ball cannot be handled in a ruck – players must try to hook the ball back with their feet so that it can be picked up by another player once it has left the ruck.

To join the ruck you must bind onto a teammate using the whole of your arm and then try to push the opposition off and away from the ball. Make sure you don't step on the player on the ground, rather try to step over him!

 In a ruck the ball is on the ground while players push to gain possession.

THE MAUL

A maul is formed when the ball is held and three or more players (at least one from each team) are bound together contesting for the ball.

To join a maul you must bind on to a teammate with your whole arm and then push the opposition back or try to wrestle the ball free so that you can either run on or pass the ball to a teammate.

It's tough in there: France's forwards drive for the line in a match against Argentina in the 2007 World Cup.

In a maul you have to wrestle with the other players to get the ball to pass on to a teammate.

TEAMWORK

When a group of players stop playing as individuals and work together to achieve a common goal, we call it teamwork. It is perhaps one of the hardest things to learn as a young player. It is easy to get the ball and run like mad until you are tackled, but, if you had slowed up a bit just before you were tackled, would that have enabled you to pass the ball to a teammate and so keep moving forwards?

You may be a wonderful rugby player, but you are unlikely to defeat an opposing team on your own. It is only by working together that you will be able to perform well and win the game.

WHAT IS GOOD TEAMWORK?
Here are some of the key things that make up good teamwork:

Communication
All members of the team should talk to one another and know what is happening around them. Players should call for the ball and communicate in defence so that there are no gaps left for the opposition to run through.

Encouragement
A good team will be full of players who encourage and support each other even when mistakes are made. No one moans or tells another player off. Only positive comments should be made.

Commitment
All members of the team work hard for each other. No one lets anyone down by not trying. Every individual player makes sure that he does his job and then looks for more to do. Everyone on the team is working towards the same goal.

Respect
All members of the team respect each other and make the effort to listen when someone has something to say.

Roles
Every player in the team knows what his role/position is and what he should do in most situations.

The ability to work as part of a team can make a big difference to how well you perform on the pitch.

LEADERSHIP

Each team needs leaders who will help guide other players towards the right decisions, enabling the team to perform at its best.

Developing leaders within the team

One way of developing leaders is to let players take responsibility for things the team does in training. Ask your coach if you or another player can lead the rest of the team in the warm up at the beginning of the next practice. You could all take turns leading five minutes of the warm up each week until players get used to taking responsibility within the team.

If the coach is agrees he may let players take control of part of the training as well, and in this way close teamwork and trust can be developed throughout the team. It is very important that the team has players who can make decisions on the field during games and help others on the team to follow those decisions. It is no use asking the coach to make the decisions. By the time they have told the team what to do from the touchline the opportunity will have passed!

Leaders

Normally, but not always, the team leaders are those that play in the spine (or backbone) of the team. This means that they are in positions which are central and therefore they can easily see and influence what is happening on the pitch.

A good captain may play on the wing and that is fine, but he will need to be able to communicate and trust players in the spine of the team to enable the team's tactics to be followed.

THE SPINE OF THE TEAM

- Hooker (no. 2)
- Number Eight (no. 8)
- Scrum Half (no. 9)
- Fly Half (no. 10)
- Fullback (no. 15)

If you look at the diagram of the team you will see why these positions are sometimes called the spine. The captain and vice captain of the team are often in one of these positions.

As players grow older, they not only grow physically, but they may also gain in confidence. This

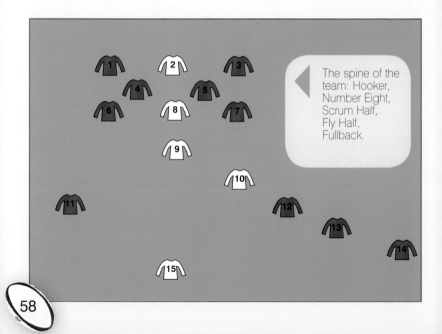

The spine of the team: Hooker, Number Eight, Scrum Half, Fly Half, Fullback.

means that a team's leaders may change from year to year and this is in itself a good thing, as the more players that have a chance to develop as leaders, the better.

The team's leaders help get everyone pulling in the same direction once the game has started, but everyone should have a good idea what tactics the team is going to use to try to win the game. Usually, the team's coach will help players decide what type of game is best suited for what the team is trying to achieve. This is called having a game plan.

DID YOU KNOW?

In the 2003 World Cup Australia scored a record-breaking number of tries in their match against Namibia. The 22 tries contributed to a phenomenal final score of 142-0.

Every team needs a leader who can make decisons quickly during a game.

TACTICS

There are a number of different ways to play the game and each team will try to out-think the other by playing to their own strengths and attempting to exploit the opposition's weaknesses.

For instance, if your team has a very good kicker as fly-half you may plan on a kicking game in your own half. This means that when the play is at your end of the field you work to get the ball to your fly half and rely on him kicking the ball deep into the opposition's half. The key will be to make sure that your players chase up quickly to force the opposition either to kick it back or to get tackled and give you a chance to win the ball back.

However, if the opposition knows that you have a fly half who is a good kicker, they might leave some of their players (their full back and perhaps wingers) deep, waiting for a kick. In that case you could run the ball and catch them unawares!

There are some basic principles of play in rugby that help us to decide which tactics to use.

PRINCIPLES OF PLAY

In rugby the rules that tell everyone how to play the game are known as laws. There are two very strange laws that make the game different from any other. The first is that you have to pass the ball backwards. If you think about it for a moment, what does this actually mean?

In other games, such as football or basketball, if you have the ball you usually pass it to your teammates in the direction you want to go to score (see diagram opposite). In rugby if we pass the ball backwards it means one of the players who has the ball has to run forwards with it, otherwise the team will end up back on its own line. It is this simple law that makes rugby a running game.

The second strange law that makes rugby very different is that once you have scored your team get the ball back!

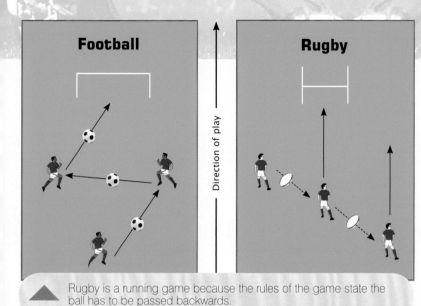

Football

Rugby

Direction of play

Rugby is a running game because the rules of the game state the ball has to be passed backwards.

Think about it – in football or basketball once you score the other team get the ball to re-start play. In rugby, the opposition have to kick it back to you. If you win the toss at the beginning of the game, you should try to keep the ball and score. Then the other team will kick it back to you, and then you can try to score again, and so on.

This usually doesn't happen, because the team with the ball will eventually make a mistake and so lose possession.

Here are some common mistakes which mean your team will lose possession of the ball:

1. Passing the ball to a member of the opposition team (an interception).

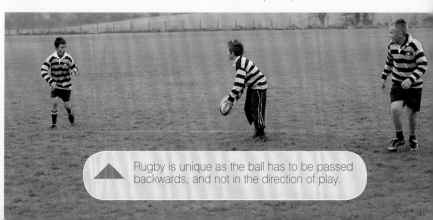

Rugby is unique as the ball has to be passed backwards, and not in the direction of play.

2. Dropping the ball and the opposition team pick it up (losing possession).
3. Passing the ball so that it goes forward (forward pass). The opposition get to put the ball into their own scrum.
4. Kicking the ball to the opposition team.
5. Running or passing the ball into touch (the side of the pitch). The opposition gets to throw the ball into a line out.
6. Committing an offence so that the opposition team is awarded a penalty (and the ball).

GAME PLANS

A team's game plan will constantly be changing as players get better at certain skills, or other circumstances change. But, simply put, the key to winning games is to enable the team to:

BE THE BEST

These are the five "principles of play" in rugby. If you understand them and remember them, it will help you be a better team player!

Name	What it means
Contest possession	Your team try to get the ball.
Go forward	You or a teammate with the ball run forwards with it.
Support	Teammates run near the ball carrier to get a backwards pass from him/her.
Continuity	Teammates keep passing and running forward without losing the ball.
Pressure	The opposing team run out of defenders and you score!

- Keep the ball as much as possible when they have possession.
- When the opposition has the ball, force them to make mistakes and therefore give the ball back.

The game plan will depend on the team's abilities and characteristics, which might include:
- Fast running backs.
- A tall set of forwards.

With these strengths the game plan could be to play a wide running or kicking game, and if the ball goes into touch, there will be a good chance of winning it again in the line out.

Players will need to react to what they see in front of them. If you have the ball and the defenders are spread out wide in front it will be a good idea to attack up the middle (see diagram 1). If the defence are bunched up then attack out wide (see diagram 2).

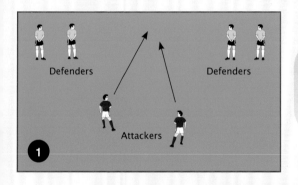

If the defence are spread out wide, it may be best to attack up the middle.

1

If you have a solid line of defence in front of you, your best option may be to attack out wide

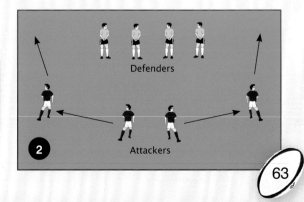

2

Bloomsbury Sport
An imprint of Bloomsbury Publishing Plc

50 Bedford Square   1385 Broadway
London   New York
WC1B 3DP   NY 10018
UK   USA
www.bloomsbury.com

Bloomsbury Sport and the Bloomsbury logo are
trademarks of Bloomsbury Publishing Plc

This edition first published 2015
© Westline Publishing, 2009, 2015

British Library Cataloguing-in-Publication Data
A catalogue record for this book is available from the
British Library.

ISBN: PB: 978-1472-9-1960-1
10 9 8 7 6 5 4 3 2 1
Typeset in the UK
Printed in China

To find out more about our authors and books visit
www.bloomsbury.com. Here you will find extracts, author
interviews, details of forthcoming events and the option to
sign up for our newsletters.

Published in 2009 as Know the Game Skills: Rugby:
Tackling, contact, teamwork, tactics and Know the Game
Skills: Rugby: Passing, catching and kicking

Photography: PA Photos, istockphoto.com
and Julia Barnes.

Special thanks to: Issy Johns-Turner, Rebecca Thompson,
Yaz Dell, Toby Webb, Carl Manley, Tom Watts, Kane Frith,
Charlie Gwyther, Ross Horman and Ben Hobbs.

Flying tackle: Mike Brown of Harlequins attempts to rein in Leinster's Rob Kearney during a Heineken Cup match at Twickenham.

About the author
Simon Jones is a level three rugby coach. He made more than 150 first team appearances for Bath. Currently, he is a trainer of coaches for the RFU (Rugby Football Union) and the IRB (International Rugby Board). A former teacher, he now runs a team of coaches delivering sport and PE in primary schools.